a Cup of Country

a Cup of Country

RAW LYRICS WAITING FOR A VOICE

SHERRY A. WRIGHT

BERONI PRODUCTIONS

Omaha, Nebraska

A CUP OF COUNTRY: RAW LYRICS WAITING FOR A VOICE
© 2023 Sherry A. Wright

This book is available through www.amazon.com and many online retailers.

For information on her other books, please visit www.BeroniProductions.com

Color Paperback: 979-8-9876352-2-3
B&W Paperback: 979-8-9876352-1-6

Design, Production and Printing through Concierge Marketing
Printed in the United States of America
10 9 8 7 6 5 4 3 2 1

Contents

Acknowledgments

L. James Wright,
Lincoln J. D. Wright
Angela L. Wright

Thank you for your support

Cover Images:
Anita Wright-Moore
L. James Wright
Mike Peklo
Mark Bertch
Rob Mason

This book is a "music on my mind" kind of thing.
What ever is on my mind, I can find it in music.

*L*yrics are written to be heard

I hope this book inspires you to take pen in hand
To write, write and rewrite.

The lyricist doesn't just use words to communicate ideas, describe scenes and tell stories. Songwriters want to send a message through their songs. We understand the power of music and words to communicate a thought. We write our songs hoping to make our audience react emotionally and physically to our words and sounds.

Perhaps these lyrics will inspire you to write and arrange your words and rhythms into forms that sound pleasing to the ear. As you write, rewrite and tweak your lyrics your words may come together in the form of lyrics/melody or melody/lyrics. The chorus may come before the Verse. And, yes even the meaning or genre may change.

The end goal is the same whether the lyric or the music comes first. In the end hopefully you will have compelling lyrics sung to a melody that entices and moves your listeners.

What ever your mood, what ever you listen to or move to, music got your back. Music is a language, the World understands. It's also true your voice is music to the ears. Why do babies cry? Why do we cry? Because we don't have the words to express what we are feeling. If we had the words to express ourselves, would we need music?

How music makes you feel is personal. My desires for what I call "Raw Lyrics" are first, to entice readers to move, feel, think or smile. And of course not only do I want to communicate ideas, describe and tell stories; I hope someone is inspired to write.

INSPIREDWORDSOUL RECIPE

Main Ingredients:
Imagination
Visualization
Lyrics
Emotions

Emotions:
Add for personal taste
Sprinkle for zest and firmness.
Add any or all of the following:
tears, insanity,
love, passion, excitement

Stir in:
Imagination, Visualization, Lyrics

Cautions:
Use care in handling. pause immediately to prevent
painful memories, personal injuries, over stimulated emotions.
There are many techniques for accomplishing this recipe.
It's not unusual for a lyricist to remix lyrics multiple
times before preconceived outcome is reached.

Patience:
Slowly simmer
You cannot rush Inspiredwordsoul Lyrics

Sharing:
Share to obtain the satisfactory results.
You will be surprised how much of your heart and soul
went into the recipe because of your efforts.

Risk:
The finished product may induce unwanted memories
May cause emotional distress
The rhythmic texture may move your body
impulsively without thought.

The easiest and quickest way to change
your mood... music, music, music.

$\mathcal{C}$OUNTRY JUST LOVE IT

WRITE IT

PRODUCE IT

INSPIRE IT

CARESS IT

BREATHE IT

ADMIRE IT

DEFEND IT

RESPECT IT

CONSOLE IT

SOOTHE IT

ENCOURAGE IT

BEHOLD IT

REMEMBER IT

SENSE IT

INHALE IT

ENHANCE IT

ACCEPT IT

EXHALE IT

SHARE IT

HONOR IT

FREE IT

ENJOY IT

SING IT

BELIEVE IT

PERFORM IT

HEAR IT

LOVE IT

IT'S COUNTRY

THANK GOD FOR IT

Pour This Man
A CUP OF COUNTRY

Verse 1:

He sat there, his head in his hands
His lady dancing with another man.
Bartender, some whiskey, mezcal or wine
The lady over there is mine.
He frowned, fumbled his keys
Bartender said, we got what you need

Chorus:

Pour this man a cup of country.
A cup of country for his jealous mind
A cup of country will work just fine
His girl just wants to dance
Not looking for romance
Don't need a shot, Just make it hot
A cup of Garth, Dolly, Brooks and Dunn
Go ahead, Go ahead, pour another one.
Pour this man a cup a cup of country

Verse 2:

She's dancing close. It's hard to bear
It's hard to watch, she knows he cares.
Steppin' and dippin', dippin' and Steppin'
She's swingin', slidin' and smilin'
The bartender nodded to the DJ
Send a cup of country, this way,

Chorus:
Pour this man a cup of country.
A cup of country for his jealous mind
A cup of country will work just fine
His girl just wants to dance
Not looking for romance
Don't need a shot, Just make it hot
A cup of Garth, Dolly, Brooks and Dunn
Go ahead, Go ahead, pour another one.
Pour this man a cup a cup of country

Verse 3:
A cup of country didn't take long
Before he was singing the song
A slow jam is beginning to play
His beautiful lady is heading his way.
This is their song, no need to fight.
He got his girl and Country tonight.

Chorus:
Pour this man a cup of country.
A cup of country for his jealous mind
A cup of country will work just fine
His girl just wants to dance
Not looking for romance
Don't need a shot, Just make it hot
A cup of Garth, Dolly, Brooks and Dunn
Go ahead, Go ahead, pour another one.
Pour this man a cup a cup of country
A cup, a cup, a cup of country.

TEXAS TUXEDO

Verse 1:
For a good Party, I'll walk a mile
Put on my smile and go out in style
Love getting down to the latest sounds
Tonight's my chance for getting down
Yeah! I be dressed , dressed to impress
Looking good, I must confessed

Chorus:
I'm a Texas tuxedo hanging around
Ready to spend my nights on the town
Hey! out of style is a misconception
It's timeless, classy, darn near perfection
Pressed blue jeans not to tight.
Bolo tie fits just right
All eyes on me like a torpedo.
Watch me, Double T. in my Texas Tuxedo

Verse 2:
Got denims pressed and bolo tie
The boots are shining, No lie
Time to go steppin' on the dance floor
Going to party like never before
Confident I'm looking sweet
This elegant Tux, is all I need

Bridge:
sophisticated gentleman, refined
attire to be admired, dressed to the nine

Chorus:
I'm a Texas tuxedo hanging around
Ready to spend my nights on the town
Hey! out of style is a misconception
It's timeless, classy, darn near perfection
Pressed blue jeans not to tight.
Bolo tie fits just right
All eyes on me like a torpedo.
Watch me, Double T, in my Texas Tuxedo

GRANDPA'S FAVORITE SONG

Verse 1:
When I was five
Grandpa took me to the park at the end of town
The bands played and the people all gathered around
Grandpa clapped and sang along
Son, that's Grandma singing my song
When I was ten Grandpa gave me Grandma's banjo
She played it at the Parkersville Fair and Rodeo

Chorus:
The smell of apple pies baking
And the sound of Grandma singing
Ending every song with I love you
Like a fairy tale come true
Grandma sang, Grandpa clapped his hands
He said I'm Grandma's number one fan
Grandpa dancing, Grandma singing
Grandpa's favorite song
Grandpa dancing, Grandma singing
Grandpa's favorite song

Verse 2:
At 18, I watch Grandpa in his old rocking chair
No pies baking, no sweet tea, Grandma wasn't there
I take Grandpa to the park at the end of town
I play Grandma's song at the old fairground
A smile, a twinkle in his eyes, Grandpa sings along.
It's my turn to play Grandpa's favorite song

Chorus:
The smell of apple pies baking
And the sound of Grandma singing
Ending every song with I love you
Like a fairy tale come true
Grandma sang, Grandpa clapped his hand
He's Grandma's number one fan
Grandpa dancing, Grandma singing
Grandpa's favorite song
Grandpa dancing, Grandma singing
Grandpa's favorite song

Music expresses that which
cannot be put into words

Time to get your music on..

Cookin' Blues

Verse 1:
I go to the store, buy food for you
Bring it home
Now, you want me to cook it too?
Take a second look
You know darn well, I don't cook.

Course:
There's a broom in the corner a pan in the sink
Something more than garbage is starting to stink.
The woman next door Grilled you a steak
The one up the street made you cupcakes.
Let them come over, cook and clean for you!
You're not giving me the Cookin' Blues
No No No,   No Cookin' Blues

Verse 2:
It came with the house,
The only reason I have a kitchen.
Baby, I'm not cookin' some dead chicken.
Get out your pots and pans.
Dead meat! Not with these hands.

Course:
There's a broom in the corner a pan in the sink
Something more than garbage is starting to stink.
The woman next door Grilled you a steak
The one up the street made you cupcakes.
Let them come over, cook and clean for you!
You're not giving me the Cookin' Blues
No No No,   No Cookin' Blues

Verse 3:
You're up all night, starting a fight.
What the heck we fighting for?
I'll go to the store, wash dirty dishes.
If you are good, I'll grant your wishes.
Turn up the heat, not from the oven
Only thing I want cookin' is your good lovin'

Chorus:
There's a broom in the corner a pan in the sink
Something more than garbage is starting to stink.
The woman next door Grilled you a steak
The one up the street made you cupcakes.
Let them come over, cook and clean for you!
You're not giving me the Cookin' Blues
No No No,   No Cookin' Blues.

(COUNTRY MAN) MORE THAN THAT

Verse 1:
I'm Country way down in my soul
Playing guitar traveling the roads
Go home to my family
A baby, a bottle, a son on my knee
Got a long leg women she waiting now for me

Chorus:
Got God's blessings right where I belong
Living my dreams, singing my songs
wearing a wide brim hat
Country, more than that.
Strong, bold and kind
Country on my mind.
Whoa, Yeah, You can call me Country,

Verse 2
Country man, singing at the game
Driving all night to get home again
The stars and stripes
I'm a Father, a Brother
Got the dreams of my Father, (Dreams of my Father)
The love, the love Oh, The love of my Mother.

Chorus:
Got God's blessings right where I belong
Living my dreams, singing my songs
wearing a wide brim hat
Country, more than that.
Strong, bold and kind
Country on my mind.
Whoa, Yeah, You can call me Country,
Yeah and More than that
I'm Country
More than that,
Country, more than that.

Another Shot of Country

Verse 1:
I cooked him a breakfast, enough for two
Steak and eggs and, a side of grits too
He didn't speak, just blew me a kiss
That's must have been some party I missed

Chorus:
He tried to stand up and sat back down
Make it hot make it strong, turn the radio on
Played till one, jammed till three
Need another shot of country
Feel more like me
Be ready for the stage tonight
The Band and the beats will be real tight
Another shot, another shot, of Country
Got to get it right.

Verse 2:
How about the hair of the dog that bit me
Concert lasted till one, we jammed till three
He stared down at the food on his plate
Wondering why he stayed out so late

Chorus:
He tried to stand up and sat back down
Make it hot make it strong, turn the radio on
Played till one, jammed till three
Need another shot of country
Feel more like me
Be ready for the stage tonight
The Band and the beats will be real tight
Another shot, another shot, of Country.
Got to get it right.

Verse 3:
He pushed the buttons on the radio
Try 92 point three, K. C. R. O.
Another gig It's Saturday night
Honey, I'll be late again tonight.

Chorus:
He tried to stand up and sat back down
Make it hot make it strong, turn the radio on
Played till one, jammed till three
Need another shot of country
Feel more like me
I'll be ready for the stage tonight
The Band and the beats will be real tight
Another shot, another shot, of Country.
Got to get it right.

CAUGHT UP

Verse 1:
Loved my job driving a big rig
Wrote a few songs played a few gigs
An agent came I signed my name
Started running looking for fame
Getting words down on the page
Yeah! Country songs are all the rage

Chorus:
Left home to be a Country Star
Guitar, duffle bag, off like a rocket
A few dollars in my pocket
Got all caught up, all caught up
Caught up in the moment
Caught in celebrations
Like so many dreamers do
Caught up, sidetracked,
Caught up can't turn back,

Verse 2:
On the road, catch me if you can
Having some fun, making new friends
Writing melodies, work never ends
We all get lost, and found again
Playing clubs and concert halls
Can't explain it, I'm having a ball

Chorus:
Left home to be a Country Star
Guitar, duffle bag, off like a rocket
A few dollars in my pocket
Now I'm caught up, I am all caught up
Caught up in the moment
Caught in celebrations
Like so many dreamers do
Caught up, sidetracked,
Can't turn back, I'm caught up

Verse 3:
There are mountains and hills to climb
Lyrics and beats run through my mind
From my rearview I steal a glance
Big rigs can't beat a song and dance
Hardly home to see my girl
I wouldn't change this life for the world

Chorus:
Left home to be a Country Star
Guitar, duffle bag, off like a rocket
A few dollars in my pocket
Now I'm caught up, I am all caught up
Caught up in the moment
Caught in celebrations
Like so many dreamers do
Caught up, sidetracked,
Can't turn back, I'm caught up.

KEY TO COUNTRY

Intro:

Ran outside to the sound of my dad's old pick-up-truck. I called Dad, Dad? My dad stepped out from behind the truck carrying an odd shaped suitcase. He said, son meet your Uncle Joe. After dinner we all went to the porch. Dad opened the odd shape case. Said, Hey Joe let's make some new memories. I was nine and from that day I started searching for Country.

Verse 1:

Asked everybody anybody where's country?
Is there someplace, anyplace I can find the key?
Called 411, checked the Yellow Pages
Checked all my maps and the GPS
Left home at 18 said I'll be back
Conductor said you're on the wrong track

Chorus:

Need a key, a key to Country,
Want to find that sound that country sound
Dad said you won't find it in the lost and found
Going to keep searching without delay
For the sound I heard on my porch that day
On my way Oklahoma, Austin, Tennessee
Somewhere, Somehow I'll find the key
Find the key to Country deep inside of me

Verse 2:

Met an old soul playing subway blues
Asked him to help me find Country to
Said, you can't find Country on an airplane
And you sure can't get there by train.
He played a country tune, the crowd cheered
You want Country, You won't find it here

Chorus:
Need a key, a key to Country,
Want to find that sound, that country sound
Dad said you won't find it in the lost and found
Going to keep searching without delay
For the sound I heard on my porch that day
On my way Oklahoma, Austin, Tennessee
Somewhere, Somehow I'll find the key
Find the key to Country deep inside of me

Verse 3:
Son, you can't find Country in a travel guide.
Packed up his guitar, we took a ride
Drove down the road, Parked near a large oak tree
Get out the Gibsons, lets find some Country
You play from your soul you have a good start
The key to Country comes from the heart

Bridge:
Hey Piano man you got the key?, (instrumental)
Hey Mason, you got the key? (instrumental)

Chorus:
Need a key, a key to Country,
Want to find that sound, that country sound
Dad said you won't find it in the lost and found
Going to keep searching without delay
For the sound I heard on my porch that day
On my way Oklahoma, Austin, Tennessee
Somewhere, Somehow I'll find the key
Find the key to Country deep inside of me.

BAD BOYS AND OUTLAWS

Verse 1:
I don't hear that country sound anymore
Had me swinging on the dance floor
I'd loved to be in that studio room
When Waylon and Merle made those tunes
They must be performing out of our view
A concert, a stage, some places new.

Chorus:
Bad boys, Bad Boys and Outlaws
From rocky roads to the hall of fame
Bring them back, bring them back again
Bad boys and Outlaws, Bad Boys and Outlaws,
Bad boys, tell me when how and where
Please tell me, how do I get there?
Waylon, Kris and Willie… Texas to Tennessee
Bad as they want to be
Bad Boys, Bad boys Bad Boys and Outlaws

Verse 2:

Where, on that radio is Cash and Merle
Don't forget country's Bad ass girls
Life is better when I tune them in
Wish they were on the road again
I checked the radio dial, where can they be?
Gee, I miss those Country harmonies.

Chorus:

Bad boys, Bad boys and Outlaws
From rocky roads to the hall of fame
Bring them back, bring them back again
Bad boys and Outlaws, Bad Boys and Outlaws,
Bad boys tell me when how and where
Please Tell me, how do I get there?
Waylon, Kris, Willie… Texas to Tennessee
Bad as they want to be
Bad Boys, Bad boys Bad Boys and Outlaws.

STIR IN SOME COUNTRY

Verse 1:
You say you love me, you say you care
You say we are the perfect pair
You can spend the night, holding me tight
Telling me baby, everything's all right

Chorus:
We can party, till the sun comes up.
(It won't do any good)
Need some country it gets me in the mood
Forget about the wine, Forget about the food
Stir some (country instrumental sounds)
Stir some (country instrumental sounds)
You got to, got to stir.... in some country

Verse 2:
Country is my life all day and night
Dancing until the morning light
There is no me, there is no you
Until you stir in some country too

Chorus:
We can party, till the sun comes up.
(It won't do any good)
Need some country it gets me in the mood
Forget about the wine, Forget about the food
Stir some (country instrumental sounds)
Stir some (country instrumental sounds)
You got to, got to stir.... in some country

Verse 3:

Buy me a truck made of silver and gold
Make a vow to have and to hold
The fact still remains. I'll explain
You and me, without country, is insane.

Chorus:

We can party, till the sun comes up.
(It won't do any good)
Need some country it gets me in the mood
Forget about the wine, Forget about the food
Stir some (country instrumental sounds)
Stir some (country instrumental sounds)
You got to, got to stir…. in some country

Let your soul speak, make music!

Hit Save, Click Return

Verse 1:
It was more than a game, It was always the same
Every time he left home on his road to fame
Dads favorite song was the one mother sang
He kissed her act like he forgot and kiss her again

Chorus:
Hit save, I'll click return
He sang loading his guitar
In the back seat of the car
"Click return" she yelled, from the doorway
"Hit save" Save that kiss till I come home
There's more where that comes from
You hit save, I'll click return

Verse 2:
Wasn't till I was older I understood why
Dad left for the road never saying goodbye
Every day before I leave I kiss my family
I click save all the hugs and kisses they give to me

Chorus:
Hit save, I'll click return
He sang loading his guitar
In the back seat of the car
"Click return" she yelled, from the doorway
"Hit save" Save that kiss till I come home
There's more where that comes from
You hit save, I'll click return

(MAY I HAVE) THIS DANCE

Intro:
Male 2: Stop day dreaming. You better go get that,
Male 3: You scared? Man, you the best dancer in the house
Male1: Yeah, And she the best dancer in the world
Male 1: Hello, May I have this Dance?

Verse 1:
I've watched you since I walked in the door
Mesmerized by you on the dance floor
A step to the right, Oh Yeah, feel that beat
A glide to the left, I am feeling the heat
Together we're in a grove
I love the way you move

Chorus:
May I have this dance, nice and slow?
Lets step step don't let go
Step step around the floor
Step step and step some more
Lets float body to body, cheek to cheek
The mood in here is getting deep
I'm glad I took a chance
To ask you for this dance

Verse 2:
Baby, you're placed just right to make that dip
It's a thermite moment with a perfect grip
When the music stops, don't walk away
We could stay right here and sway, sway, sway
How about another one
You make it so much fun.

Chorus:
May I have this dance, nice and slow?
Let's step step don't let go
Step step around the floor
Step step and step some more
Let's float body to body, cheek to cheek
The mood in here is getting deep
I'm glad I took a chance
To ask you for this dance.

$\mathcal{I}$ ONLY LOVE YOU WHEN

Verse 1:
I only love you when you come into view
And every time I think of you.
In my dreams In every way
Each God given moment …Each God given day
Whenever I am hungry, when I eat
Every time my heart beats
With every breath I take,
When I sleep, when I awake

Chorus:
There's something I need you to know
Tomorrows come and tomorrows goes
Minutes turn to hours and hours to days
Our love is not just another cliche
I only love, love you when,
Trees dance in the wind
When the grass is green, the sky is blue
I only love you when, I only love you,
............When

Verse 2:

I love you when I open or close my eyes
Every sunset…every sunrise
When I hear the music
Of a bird, the wind or a sweet melody
When I write In the middle of the night
When you're holding me tight
When I lay down to sleep
Pray the Lord…our love to keep

Chorus :

There's something I need you to know
Tomorrows come and tomorrows goes
Minutes turn to hours and hours to days
Our love is not just another cliche
I only love, love you when,
Trees dance in the wind
When the grass is green, the sky is blue
I only love you when, I only love you,
.... When.

WE DIDN'T KNOW

Verse 1: (Female)
We shot hoops, camped out, picnicked with your folks
Laughed at your fathers funny jokes
We did our homework after school
Swam in the neighborhood pool.

Chorus: (Male & Female)
We were always the best of friends
Didn't know one day it would end
Never noticed, time past us by
Never asked when, never asked why
     (Male)
I didn't know, who would ever guess
You left for college, I was a mess
(Male & Female)
We didn't know, We didn't know
I loved you, It's true I love you too.
We didn't know

Verse 2: (Male)
I missed you and I often reminisce
the day we had our first kiss
I thought our lives would never change
Didn't know until I felt the pain.

Chorus: (Male & Female)
We were always the best of friends
Didn't know one day it would end
Never noticed, time past us by
Never asked when, never asked why
       (Male)
I didn't know, who would have ever guessed
I didn't notice, I must confess
          (Male & Female)
We didn't know, We didn't know
I loved you, It's true I love you too.
We didn't know

GOD TOLD ME ABOUT YOU

Verse 1:
Must have been an angel
Who whispered in my ear
Your time for love is near
There's someone especially for you
Prayers and dreams do come true.
Because, because

Chorus:
God told me, told me about you
A Heavenly seed grows in my heart
A promise, never to part.
He has a plan and I believe it
He's prepared me to receive it
God told me, told me about you
God told me, told me about you

Verse 2:
Must have been an angel
Said you were created with love
Chosen from His Garden above
He said you have a caring heart,
I'll love you right from the start
Because, because

Chorus:
God told me, told me about you
A Heavenly seed grows in my heart
A promise, never to part.
He has a plan and I believe it
He's prepared me to receive it
God told me, told me about you
God told me, told me about you

Verse 3:
Must have been an Angel
Brought me God's message
And a gift made in His image
God is a great Artist, It's true
I can see His work in you
Because, because

Chorus:
God told me, told me about you
A Heavenly seed grows in my heart
A promise, never to part.
He has a plan and I believe it
He's prepared me to receive it
God told me, told me about you
God told me, told me about you

Heaven's Tours

Verse 1:
There's a place Jesus prepared for me
A Heavenly home I'd love to see
To sit and learn from the apostles
About Love according to the gospel

Chorus:
When Heaven opens for public tours
I'll listen to choir voices, so pure
No need for coats, hats or gloves
Everyone is surrounded with love
Before I leave I'll take time to pray
In a place I'll call home someday
It will be all I imagine and more
When Heaven opens for public tours

Verse 2:
A Heavenly tour, I can't resist
The Garden of Eden, first on my list
I can't see it all in just one visit
No credit needed Jesus has my ticket

Chorus:
When Heaven opens for public tours
I'll listen to choir voices, so pure
No need for coats, hats or gloves
Everyone is surrounded with love
Before I leave I'll take time to pray
In a place I'll call home someday
It will be all I imagine and more
When Heaven opens for public tours

Verse 3:

I'll ride moon beans through the Streets of gold
Walk where mysteries and wisdom unfold
View Peaks and Valleys where God carries man
Leaving one set of footprints in the sand

Chorus:

When Heaven is open for public tours
I'll listen to choir voices, so pure
No need for coats, hats, or gloves
Everyone is surrounded with love
Before I leave I'll take time to pray
In a place I'll call home someday
It will be all I imagine and more
When Heaven opens for public tours

DOWN IN THE WATER

Mama always told me, I needed to get right with the Lord.
Told me He will get you through. She sang her praises never forgetting
where her blessings came from. That's why...

Verse 1:
That's why
I went down in the water and now I want to sing
I went down in the water and now I want to sing
I went down in the water   singing
Halle -lu Halle- lu …Hal - le -luuuu -jah

I went down in the water, found amazing grace
I went down in the water, found amazing grace
I went down in the water, And
Now,   now I see

Chorus:
Went in the water and now I'm found
I believed and turned my life around.
Because I went down, down, down
In the water
I feel it, feel it in my soul
I hear it, hear it in my song,
Because I went down, down, down
In the water

Verse 2:
I went down in the water and I got joy
I went down in the water and I got joy
I went down in the water
I got joy, joy, joy, joy

I went down in the water to cleanse my soul
I went down in the water to cleanse my soul
I went down in the water,
My sins washed away

Chorus:
Went in the water and now I'm found,
I believed and turned my life around.
Because I went down, down, down
In the water
I feel it in my soul, in my soul
I hear it in my song, in my song
Because I went down, down, down
In the water

Verse 3:
I went down in the water to praise Him
I went down in the water to praise Him
I went down in the water,
Now I am right with   the Lord

I went down in the water now I want to shout
I went down in the water now I want to shout
I went down in the water,   Shouting
Amen, Amen,   Amen…

Chorus:
Went in the water and now I'm found,
I believed and turned my life around.
Because I went down, down, down
In the water
I feel it in my soul, in my soul
I hear it in my song, in my song
Because I went down, down, down
In the water

It is time to put a voice
to those Raw Lyrics

THANKS FOR THE JOURNEY

Verse 1:
Thanks for the sunshine and the rain.
Giving me comfort through tears and pain.
Blessing me with peace after sleepless nights,
Touched me, making everything all right.

Chorus:
Thank You for my journey. My journey home.
You chose me from Your sacred place
Gave me gifts, blessings and amazing grace,
You know my mind and my heart
You've been with me from the start
Your work in me is from above
Your heavenly tool is love
Thank You for my journey home

Verse 2:
You saved me saved me from a fall
Lifted me up every time I call
Taught me wisdom, led me on my way
Grace and mercy teaching me to pray

Chorus:
Thank You for my journey. My journey home.
You chose me from Your sacred place
Gave me gifts, blessings and amazing grace,
You know my mind and my heart
You've been with me from the start
Your work in me is from above
Your heavenly tool is love
Thank You for my journey home

(YOU ARE) THAT SOMEONE

Verse 1:

I ran into a friend I hadn't seen in a while
He still lights up a room with his contagious smile
He asked me about my life and family
As we sipped coffee in the Olsen Deli
He asked if I was married or seeing someone
I said there's only one I haven't overcome

Chorus:

You're that one, that got away
The reason for words I can't seem to say
The one I have not overcome
You are, you are that someone
If I tell you the words I find hard to say
If I tell you, will you still walk away
The one I have not overcome
You are, you are that someone

Verse 2:

He fell in love thinks of her now and then
I quickly changed the topic to old times and friends
He looked at his watch said he had to go
I felt something stirring deep in my soul
I hoped he'd walk away before he saw me cry
We stood, hugged and said goodbye

Chorus:

You're that one, that got away
The reason for words I can't seem to say
The one I have not overcome
You are, you are that someone
If I tell you the words I find hard to say
If I tell you, will you still walk away
The one I have not overcome
You are, you are that someone
You are, you are that someone

WHEN YOU SAY GOODBYE

Intro:
What am I going to do, when you say goodbye
    What am I going to do, when you leave me?

Verse 1:
Remember the first time I looked into your eyes
Loved you from that moment, I can't tell you why
For a while we lived in paradise
Now you're asking me to apologize

Chorus:
What do I do when you say goodbye
What do I do when you leave me
It's not about who's wrong or right
The beginning, the ending, or the fight
The hardest part is unable to touch
And loving, loving, loving you too much
When you leave I'll just smile and say goodbye
There will be no tears falling from these eyes
When you say,   say goodbye

Verse 2:
I Can't say I'm sorry for the thing I've done
I Can't say I'm sorry you're the only one
Or believing our love would last
I'm not sorry for the present or the past

Chorus:
What do I do when you say goodbye
What do I do when you leave me
It's not about who's wrong or right
The beginning, the ending or the fight
The hardest part is unable to touch
And loving, loving, loving you too much
When you leave I'll just smile and say goodbye
There will be no tears falling from these eyes
When you say,   say goodbye

Verse 3:
It's only my situation I'll rectify
There's no need to justify or clarify
Words won't be hard for me to convey
I'm not going to beg you to stay

Chorus:
What do I do when you say goodbye
What do I do when you leave me
It's not about who's wrong or right
The beginning, the ending or the fight
The hardest part is unable to touch
And loving, loving, loving you too much
When you leave I'll just smile and say goodbye
There will be no tears falling from my eyes
When you say,   say goodbye

Do DROP INN

Intro:
Ringing...Ringing...
Sorry I'm not available to take your call

Verse 1:
You can leave a message after the beep
You never call to say you'll be late
If you want to see me I'll be downtown
It's a par-taa, I'm getting down

Chorus:
Baby, I'm gone. I cancelled the date
You said you'd call half past eight
It's a heck of a party at the Do Drop Inn
I'm getting down and drinking gin
Kickin' boots, making new friends
Down at the Do Drop Inn

I came to party, having a ball
I Won't be home before Last Call
Music jamming got a honky-tonk groove
I'm getting down, learning new moves
Hey! Hey! It's a party at the Do Drop Inn

Chorus:
Baby, I'm gone. I cancelled the date
You said you'd call half past eight
It's a heck of a party at the Do Drop Inn
I'm getting down and drinking gin
Kickin' boots, making new friends
Down at the Do Drop Inn
Do Drop, Do Drop, Do Drop In

Outro: Answering machine

DREAMS

Intro: Speak
I take this woman to be my wife
To love and to cherish for the rest of my life?

Verse 1:
Last night I dreamed of rivers and oceans
Become a body of one.
I dreamed we declared our love
As we watched from the banks above

Chorus:
When I lay down to sleep I dream of you
What seems like a fairy tale come true
Today I watch clouds in the sky
Like Heaven's angels floating by
Reminds me of my love for you.
Is it just a dream, Could it be true?

Verse 2:
Today I found the Rainbow's end
All I dreamed, all I ever imagined
Today, I wait in awe of you
At the end of the aisle to say I do

Chorus:
When I lay down to sleep I dream of you
What seems like a fairy tale come true
Today I watch clouds in the sky
Like Heaven's angels floating by
Reminds me of my love for you.
Is it just a dream, Could it be true?

Close your eyes...Smile...
Tap your fingers...write
You got rhythm.

CAN I SNEAK A PEEK

Verse 1:

Hello, I know we just met
We hadn't been introduced yet
I'm hoping you want to know me to
If it's a matter of trust I don't blame you
What is it you want to do or say
Can I help you in any way

Chorus:

I respect and understand your privacy
What's in my heart I only allow you to see
What's a man got to do
To get to know you
What is it you aspire,
What is it you desire
Baby just a little taste a little peek
Baby can I, can I please, sneak a peek

Verse 2:
Is there a special someone
Can I get your 411
What do you need what is it you want
What is your motivation
Just a little hint, a little lead
Give me a peek won't you please

Chorus:
I respect and understand your privacy
What's in my heart I only allow you to see
What's a man got to do
To get to know you
What is it you aspire,
What is it you desire
Baby just a little taste a little peek
Baby can I, can I please, sneak a peek

I AM A TREE

Verse 1:
He's so smart, barely three
He'd raises his hands pretending to be a tree
I am a tree blowing in the wind
waving his hands in the air
Reaching up, waving his little fingers
Up, up and down
Touching his fingers to the ground

Chorus:
I am a tree blowing in the wind
I am the rain falling on the grass
A song my grandson sings with me
I am a tree blowing in the wind
I am the rain falling on the grass
I especially love the part
I'm a big boy, Love is in my heart.

Verse 2:
Today we're the wind and the rain
It is a song, It's a game.
Tomorrow a rainbow in the sky
A Man in the moon, my grandson and I
Somedays he is a bird in a tree
He's only two, not even three.

Chorus:
I am a tree blowing in the wind
I am the rain falling on the grass
A song my grandson sings with me
I am a tree blowing in the wind
I am the rain falling on the grass
I especially love the part
I'm a big boy, Love is in my heart.

COMPASSION

Verse 1:
There are messages of love all around us
It's the wars and hate we are most conscious
We are masters of our own fate
Let's get together before it's too late.
We keep calling for peace and all men's rights,
Yet we chose our weapons and prepare to fight.

Chorus:
There are needs we can't see
Have compassion, show some sensitivity
How can we offer peace to someone else
When we do not practice it ourselves?
It only takes one to change someone's condition
Common decency and Compassion
Life is not a spectator sport, what do we gain
watching, cheering, causing pain

Verse 2:
A young child is dead another paralyzed.
Tell me, What does it take to realize
Are we so in-compassionate
As we watch while a few incite hate
Let's Put unity in humanity.
We could do away with the silent apathy.

Bridge:
Motivate, encourage, recognize, Take action
That's how we show compassion

Chorus:
There are needs we can't see
Have compassion, show some sensitivity
How can we offer peace to someone else
When we do not practice it ourselves?
It only takes one to change someone's condition
Common decency and Compassion
Life is not a spectator sport, what do we gain
watching, cheering, causing pain

COULDN'T SEE THE FOREST FOR THE TREES

Verse 1:
Not long ago the bars were my playground
Hanging with the boys, nights on town
There was Jodi, Mary Lou and Party time
Lots and lots of Whisky, Gin and wine.

Me and the boys, cheering at the ball games
You came along, now nothing seem the same.
You showed me the trees standing tall
Now, I love you, love you most of all

Chorus:
I couldn't see the forest for the trees
Living life, running free (Living life running free)
I couldn't see the forest for the trees
I couldn't see the forest for the trees
This is now, that was then.
You showed me trees, dancing in the wind

Verse 2:
My family all came to meet my new friend
With trees, dancing in the wind
We sat in the backyard, having fun.
Whispering in my ear, she's the one.

Uncle Charley said, Son, you got it right.
He said the trees are bowing down tonight.
You've always been a ladies man
You better catch her if you can.

Chorus:
I couldn't see the forest for the trees
Living life, running free (Living life running free)
Couldn't see the forest for the trees
Couldn't see the forest for the trees
This is now, that was then.
You showed me trees, dancing in the wind

Verse 3:
My Dad told me, he married his best friend
Under the trees dancing in the Wind
With trees reaching for the sky
Son, Don't let love pass you by

I'm passing up the nights on the town
Not missing all the old playgrounds
I see more than forest and trees
You are the tree, you are the breeze.

Chorus:
I couldn't see the forest for the trees
Living life, running free (Living life running free)
Couldn't see the forest for the trees
Couldn't see the forest for the trees
This is now, that was then.
You showed me trees, dancing in the wind

Sing like everyone
is listening.

A RADIO AND A ROCKIN' CHAIR

Verse :1

I'm sitting here with you next to your bed
Wondering if we left any thing unsaid
You have memories inside you can't express
I miss you, I miss you I must confess

Chorus:

I brought your radio and rockin' chair
To remind you of the things we share
I'm hoping you'll hear and understand
The sounds of the radio, the touch of my hand
I'll be the voice of your hopes and dreams
You will always be my rockin' chair queen

Verse :2

I use the blanket from your rockin' chair
To hug my shoulders as if you were still there.
Laughing at my jokes sipping sweet tea
This radio and rockin' chair means so much to me

Chorus:

I brought your radio and rockin' chair
To remind you of the things we share
I'm hoping you'll hear and understand
The sounds of the radio, the touch of my hand
I'll be the voice of all your hopes and dreams
You will always be my rockin' chair queen

Your Notes

Change your music...Change your mood.

It's all about the music...

Never underestimate the power of music....

Listen to your heart,
Listen to your soul

Write. Write. Rewrite.

Music, is it music or magic?

www.ingramcontent.com/pod-product-compliance
Lightning Source LLC
Chambersburg PA
CBHW022039090426
42741CB00007B/1122